How to Stay Healthy

Written by Helen Jaeger

AUTUMN
PUBLISHING

Written by Helen Jaeger
Illustrated by Anne Passchier

Designed by Richard Sykes
Edited by Helen Catt

Copyright © 2021 Igloo Books Ltd

Published in 2021
First published in the UK by Autumn Publishing
An imprint of Igloo Books Ltd
Cottage Farm, NN6 0BJ, UK
Owned by Bonnier Books
Sveavägen 56, Stockholm, Sweden

All rights reserved, including the right of reproduction
in whole or in part in any form.

Manufactured in China. 1021 001
10 9 8 7 6 5 4 3 2 1

Library of Congress Cataloging-in-Publication
Data is available upon request.

ISBN 978-1-83903-669-9
autumnpublishing.co.uk
bonnierbooks.co.uk

Includes **EXERCISE PLANNER** poster

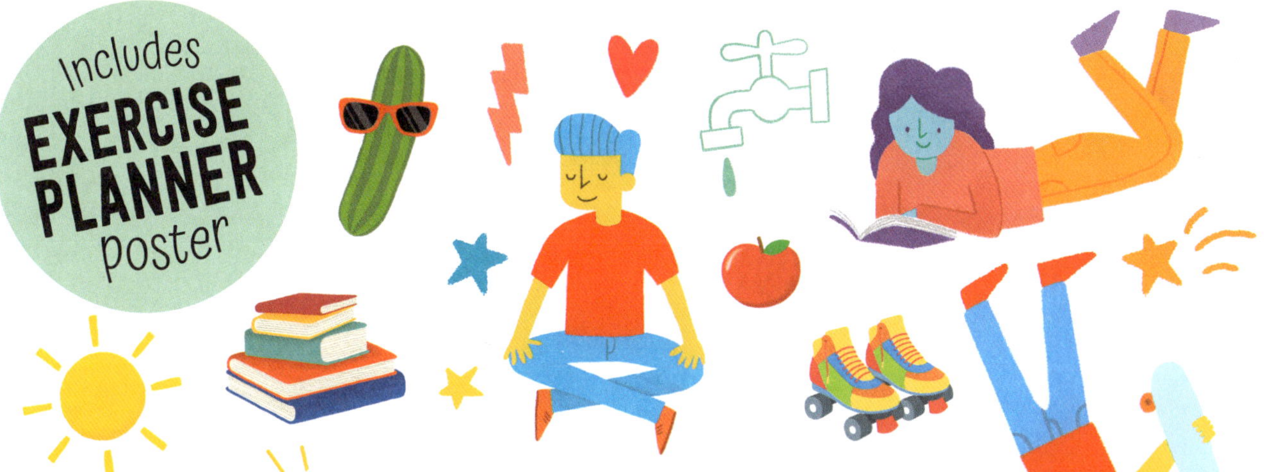

How to STAY HEALTHY

Written by Helen Jaeger

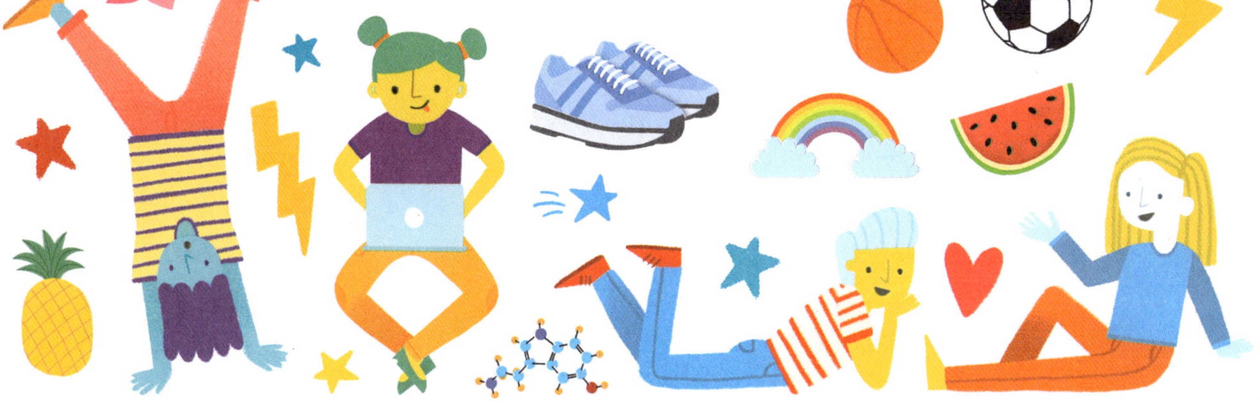

iNTRODUCTiON

HEY!

Good job for picking up this book! You're about to start on an exciting journey to a healthy you! There are lots of spaces for you to write and draw in. Make this book YOUR OWN! If you  what you see, why not share it with an adult, too?

x

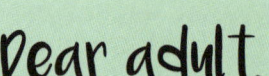

Dear adult,

Welcome to this book about healthy kids. As a Mom and a children's well-being practitioner, I know how tough the pressures on children are. In my book, you'll find a range of ways to get and stay healthy, from lunch-box ideas to how to encourage good sleep. There are lots of activities children can do by themselves or with you. You can give this book to your child to use as a journal or you could work on ideas together. Whatever you do, I wish you a healthy family life!

Helen Jaeger

CONTENTS

Your body is amazing!	6
I like to move it!	8
Who's with you?	10
Special family fun	12
Mix it up	14
Delish combos	16
Grow your own	18
Wonderful water!	19
What happens when you sleep?	20
Go outside	22
Body scanning	24
Going to the doctor	26
Going to the dentist	28
Going to the optometrist	30
Going to hospital	32
Taking medicines	34
HELP!!! 911	36
Basic first aid	38
Bad for bodies: cigarettes	40
Bad for bodies: alcohol	42
Disability	44
Wonderful me	46
Help! (resources)	48

YOUR BODY IS AMAZING!

Can you draw a full-length picture of yourself? Include as much detail as you can! Then name as many body parts as you can.

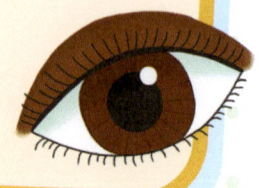

Look what you can do!

Each part of your body has an important job to do, even the really little parts. Did you know doctors can tell if you are ill just by the color of your fingernails, or whether you have problems with your heart by looking into your eyes? Some parts of our bodies we can see. Some are hidden away inside us.

Can you think why your eyelashes are important? And your toes? Our bodies really are amazing! That's why it's important to look after them.

What jobs do these body parts do?

Eyes:

Ears:

Nose:

Mouth:

Fingers:

Hair:

Heart:

Stomach:

Intestines:

Lungs:

Muscles:

Joints:

Spine:

Skull:

Skin:

i like to move it!

Our bodies love to move. Moving does us good. That's why it's important we keep active. But we don't all have to do the same thing. Some people like to walk and others like to dance. Your best friend might love gymnastics, but you prefer football. The important thing is to find ways of moving that you find fun!

How many of these have you tried?
Circle the activities you've tried below.

walking   dancing   gymnastics   swimming   football
skateboard   scooter   running   bicycling   volleyball
athletics   rugby   hockey   ice-skating   rowing
paddleboarding   canoeing   tennis   basketball
baseball   trampolining   bowling   roller-skating
circuits   catch   tag   skipping   dodgeball
dog-walking   surfing   climbing
tidying   gardening

Are there any other activities you would like to try?
Write them here:

Why activity matters!

Which of these sentences do you think are true? Put a check mark next to the ones you think are correct.

When we are active, blood moves more quickly around our bodies. ☐

Moving around helps our muscles grow strong. ☐

Being active can help us to stay calm. ☐

Being active helps us to concentrate. ☐

Being active improves our eyesight and hearing. ☐

Being active means we're less likely to get sick. ☐

Being active helps us to relax and sleep better. ☐

Moving around is good for our mental and emotional health. ☐

Being active is fun. ☐

Guess what? They're all true! No matter how young or old we are, our bodies reward us when we move around by making us feel good. That's because being active helps our bodies. It's our bodies' way of saying thank you!

> Why not make a promise to your body that you will keep moving around? Think of all the rewards you'll get!

Dear Body,

I promise to be active.
Thanks for the rewards, like better sleep, feeling happy, and being strong.

Signed:_____

Who's With You?

Luckily, you don't have to rely on other people to be active. Circle the activities below where you DON'T need a sports buddy. Which are your faves? Give them a go. There's nothing stopping you!

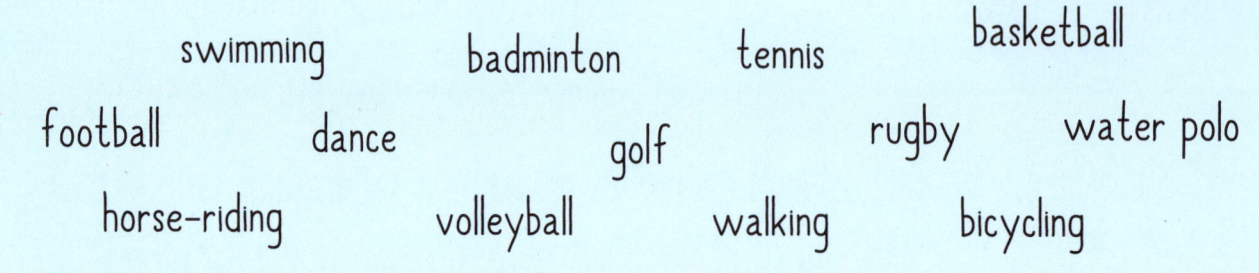

swimming   badminton   tennis   basketball
football   dance   golf   rugby   water polo
horse-riding   volleyball   walking   bicycling

TOP TIP!

Even if you think you can't do a sport like rugby or basketball alone, maybe you can! Remember, you don't need a team to practice the skills, like finding the back of a net or hitting a tennis ball against a wall.

Basketball legend, Michael Jordan, needed to improve his jump shots, so he spent an entire off-season practicing them.

And you don't need the best kit! Serena Williams, world tennis champ, grew up playing on gritty, cracked tennis courts.

GET GOING!

10

Team YEAH!

Of course, if you would prefer to do sports with others, you don't have to look far. Maybe your school or a local activity group run sports sessions? After-school clubs often center around sports. Ask around, too, especially if you're nervous about a first session. Going with someone else can make it easier.

No luck? Do an internet search for your local area, or ask an adult to help you. You may be surprised by what you find.

If you don't want to join a club, that's fine, too. Perhaps you and your best friend share a passion for dance? Or football? Invite your friends over for some fun sports activities or do it together online.

Ultimate team

Now's your chance to create your dream squad! Who would you have in it and what sport would you play? Draw your team in the box! You can include celebs, your fave sports stars, and your friends and family, too!

Switch things up and, most of all, have FUN! If you enjoy something, you're more likely to keep doing it.

SPECIAL FAMILY FUN

Maybe members of your family enjoy being active, too. After all, there are lots of ways to be sporty with other people, and lots of places to do it!

Name an activity you could do in each of the below locations. There are some ideas underneath.

In the house: _____
In the yard: _____
At the park: _____
At the beach: _____
In the woods: _____
At the lake: _____
At the pool: _____

IDEAS:

hide-and-seek   sardines   cricket   fly a kite

football   tag   swim   play leapfrog

gymnastics   dance   thumb wars   build a fort

build a sandcastle   baseball

canoe

running races   handstands

12

Make a simple kite!

You will need:

- ◆ 8.5 x 11 piece of cardstock
- ◆ Twine
- ◆ Stapler
- ◆ Pencil
- ◆ Ruler
- ◆ Hole punch
- ◆ Toilet roll tube

Instructions

1. Fold your cardstock in half.
2. Turn the cardstock so the fold is closest to you.
3. Measure 6 cm from the left side and mark it (A).
4. Measure another 6 cm from this point and mark it (B).
5. Take one corner up to the first mark, so it forms a sort of tube. Don't crease it down.
6. Do the same with its opposite corner.
7. Where these two ends meet, staple together onto the main body of the kite.
8. Punch a hole where you made the second mark and hook twine through it.
9. You can wind the twine around an empty toilet roll tube to make it easier to fly.

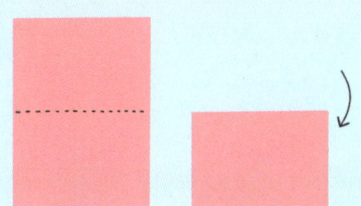
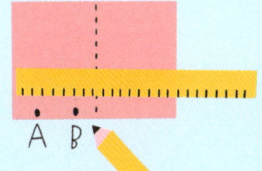
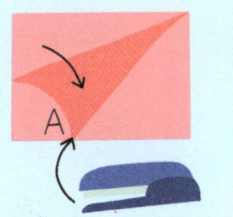

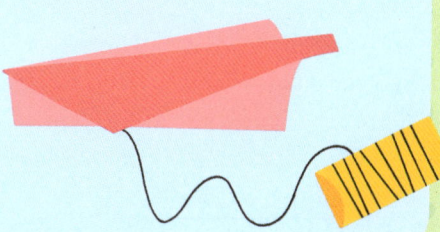

Mix it Up

To be healthy, we all need to get a mix of different foods. Here's how you can split your food up to make sure you're getting everything your body needs.

Veggies — Fill half your plate with veggies and fruit!

Fruit — Sweet and good for you!

Dairy — For strong teeth and bones!

Don't forget water!

Protein — Helps you grow healthy!

Grains — These fill you up!

14

your healthy lunch box

Fill up the lunch box below by drawing some of your favorite fresh snacks. You can use the ideas below.

Salad or veggies
Cucumber, cherry tomatoes, fresh spinach, roasted peppers, carrot sticks... the list goes on!

Fruit salad
Mix up your faves. Add honey for extra sweetness.

You can add seeds or nuts, too! Sesame and poppy seeds are yummy!

Sandwich or wrap
(see next page!)

Yogurt

15

DELISH COMBOS

One great way to get all the healthy food you need is to put it in a wrap. Wholewheat is best! Here are some ideas for you. Draw lines from your faves onto the wrap to build your ideal recipe, then have a go at making it!

MEAT ham, turkey, chicken pieces

VEGGIES carrots, shredded beets, sweetcorn, peppers

EGG hard-boiled and chopped

FISH tuna, salmon, smoked mackerel, shrimp

SALAD lettuce, spinach leaves, cherry tomatoes, cucumber, cress

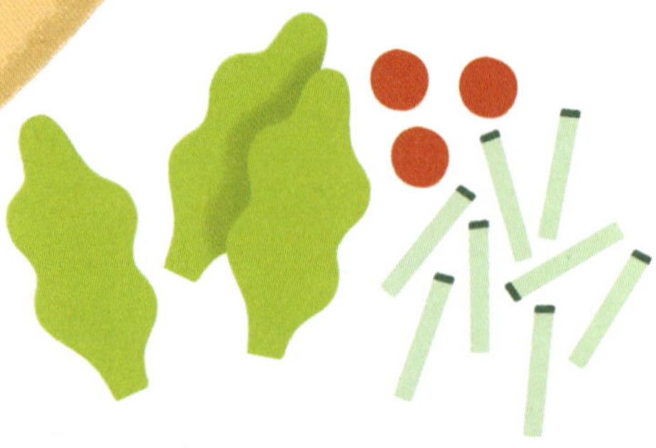

CHEESE cheddar, feta, or your fave!

'SAUCE' guacamole, mayo, salad dressing

FRUIT FOR DESSERT apple, orange, grapes

You could make a healthy bowl of food and add nuts/seeds, too!

16

Super smoothies!

Here's another great way to get healthy. Smoothies are fantastic with breakfast or after school, too. You'll need a blender. Ask an adult to help.

MILK OR WATER Make sure there's enough to make it drinkable. You can use non-dairy milks (oat, coconut, almond or soy) if you prefer.

OATS OR CHIA SEEDS This will give you long-lasting energy and make the smoothie nice and thick.

FRUIT Frozen raspberries, blueberries, strawberries, and bananas work well, but use whatever you like!

VEGGIES You can stick a few spinach or kale leaves in for a health kick. You won't notice they're there!

SEEDS Add a few seeds like sesame or sunflower for extra goodness.

SWEETENER Add a little honey or syrup for sweetness. Taste before you add. It might not need it!

1. Blend.
2. Add more water or milk if needed.
3. ENJOY!

Try these combos!

Pumpkin spice:
Mix a can of unsweetened pumpkin puree with cinnamon and spices, mashed banana, a tiny dash of maple syrup, and milk.

Fresh and zingy:
Whizz up a good handful of spinach with the juice of half a lime, some ginger, a few sprigs of mint, and some pineapple or some kiwi fruit. Top it up with apple juice or coconut milk.

Peachy pink:
Mash bananas, peaches, a dash of vanilla extract, and some Greek yogurt. Top it off with milk, and if you like, sprinkle in some chia seeds. If you decide to use chia seeds, let the mixture chill for a few hours to soften before drinking.

GROW YOUR OWN

Did you know you can grow your own veggies and salad? Perhaps you have a parent or grandparent who grows their own?

If you want to grow your own, try this do-it-yourself.

CHIA HEAD

You will need:
egg, markers, egg box, cotton, chia seeds.

1. Ask an adult to boil an egg. Eat up, being careful not to crack the shell too much. Clean the inside with warm water.

2. Decorate your empty eggshell with a face or patterns.

3. Stand the egg shell in egg tray.

4. Fill the egg shell with cotton up to 1 cm from the top.

5. Sprinkle chia seeds onto the cotton.

6. Mist or gently water the seeds.

7. Place the seeds on a sunny windowsill if you have one. Mist or gently water a little every day. Within 10 days you should have your very own chia head!

WHAT NEXT?

Give your chia head a "haircut" and add it to salads, omelettes, and wraps.

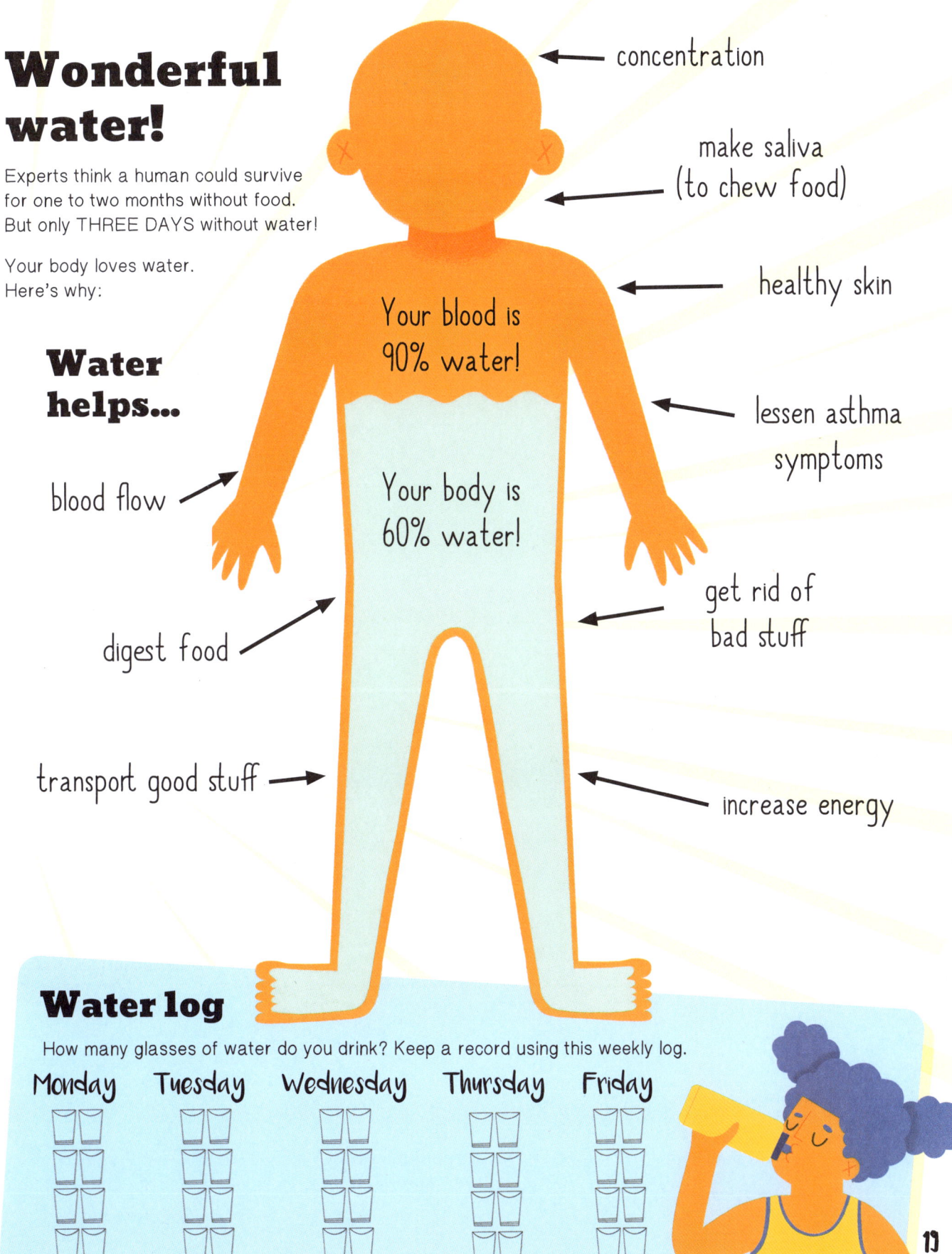

What happens when you sleep?

Repair, restore, and reenergize. Sleep is so good for your whole body! Here are some of the good things from getting lots of zzzzzzs.

Sleep helps...

- sharpen problem-solving skills
- fight infection
- better decisions
- your brain process info
- increase energy
- your body relax
- store memories
- fade stress
- you grow
- you be more creative
- you focus better
- you feel happier
- heal injuries

How much sleep do I need?

Think you're getting enough sleep? Here's what experts say...

☾ **birth to 3 months:** 14 to 17 hours

☾ **4 to 12 months:** 12 to 16 hours per 24 hours, including naps

☾ **1 to 2 years:** 11 to 14 hours per 24 hours, including naps

☾ **3 to 5 years:** 10 to 13 hours per 24 hours, including naps

☾ **6 to 12 years:** 9 to 12 hours

☾ **13 to 18 years:** 8 to 10 hours

☾ **18 to 60 years:** 7 or more hours

☾ **61 to 64 years:** 7 to 9 hours

☾ **65 years and older:** 7 to 8 hours

MAKE YOUR OWN SLEEP CLOCK

It's easy to be distracted by games and phones and, before you know it, you're not getting enough sleep. If you find yourself waking up the next day tired, grumpy, and unfocused, this sleep clock is for you!

You will need: paper plate, card, markers, split pin (brad), skewer

1 Cut the colored card into a circle that's a bit smaller than the paper plate.

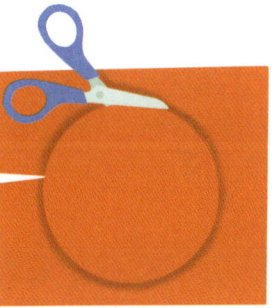

2 Cut a quarter out of the colored card, leaving a little bit in the middle.

3 Write "time to bed" and "time to get up" on the cut edges of the card.

4 Mark the hours (1-12) around the edge of the paper plate.

5 Lay the card over the paper plate and make a hole that goes through the middle of both.

6 Insert the split pin (brad) You should be able to move the inner ¾ disc over the top of the paper plate.

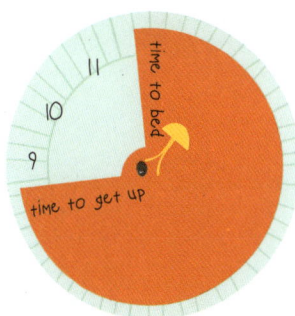

To use: Move the arrow "time to bed" to your desired time. Check out what the "time to get up" arrow is pointing to. This is your earliest get-up! Or, if you have to get up at a certain time, line the "time to get up" arrow with that time and check what time you should go to bed. This is your latest go-to-bed!

GO OUTSIDE

It's great for your health to get out and about in nature. Visit a park or some woods and make this den or hideout. You can use it as shelter or as a "hide" to watch wildlife without disturbing it.

1 Find a tree with a low-hanging branch. This is the base of your roof.

2 Gather bigger sticks to lean up against the branch to form a triangular shape. Fill in gaps with smaller sticks.

3 Use plants like bracken to cover over any gaps. Then sprinkle dry leaves to make a comfy floor for your den.

Being in nature is good for your sleep patterns. Unplug from your computer before bed, and go outside instead to listen to birdsong or watch the stars.

Just take a walk

When you go for a walk, what do you notice? Maybe you've heard birdsong or a running stream? Perhaps sunlight bouncing off a river caught your eye? You might have hugged a tree or run your fingers down its rough, crinkled bark.

If you stick your tongue out, sometimes you can taste the fresh air. Or you enjoy the smell of fresh-cut grass. Next time you go for a walk, remember to use ALL your senses. It will make you enjoy your walk even more.

Take this book out with you and answer these questions.

What can I see?

What can I hear?

What can I feel?

What can I smell?

Can I taste anything?

Now write a few sentences about how you feel. Are you happy? Sad? Calm? Take time to really notice your feelings.

23

BODY SCANNING

Ever been to an airport and had your luggage scanned? This time you're going to scan your body. It's a handy way to get immediate relaxation.

What to do:

- Lie down on the floor and close your eyes.
- Relax your body as much as you can.
- Scrunch up your toes as hard as you can and relax.
- Tense your leg muscles and relax.
- Squeeze your butt cheeks together and relax.
- Tense your back and relax.
- Tense your tummy and relax.
- Tense your shoulders and relax.
- Tense your arms and relax.
- Scrunch up your hands and relax.
- Clench your jaw and relax.
- Scrunch up your face and relax.
- Frown as hard as you can and relax.
- Squeeze your eyes tight shut and relax.
- Now let your body sink into the floor.
- Do this as many times as you like!

MORE RELAXATION TIPS

Slow your breathing

Imagine you're holding a mug of hot chocolate (yum!). Breathe OUT to cool it down and IN to smell it.

Say something kind to yourself

Repeat an "affirmation" to yourself. These are positive statements that you can say to help give yourself a boost. Here are some ideas.

- ♥ I am safe.
- ♥ I am loved.
- ♥ I am kind.
- ♥ I am important.

Come up with your own affirmation and write it below. What would you like to tell yourself?

If you're stuck, imagine what kind things you would like to say to a friend, and try saying them to yourself.

Affirmation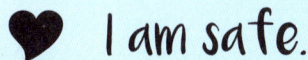

Imagine a place that makes you happy. It could be a real place or an imaginary place. Draw it here.

25

GOING TO THE DOCTOR

Sometimes when we feel sick, medicine at home doesn't help. Doctors find out what is wrong with us and give us medicine to make us better. If they can't help, they know other experts who can.

1 Your adult will make an appointment for you with your doctor, usually over the phone or online.

2 You will go with your adult to the doctors' office, where the doctors work.

4 You might have to wait. There may be other people there. But the receptionist will tell you when you can go in, or your name might come up on a screen so you know it's your turn.

3 When you get to the office, a receptionist will say hello. They will take your details and let the doctor know you are here.

5 The doctor will greet you in their own room. It is private. Your grown-up can come in with you.

6 The doctor will examine you and ask questions to find out what is wrong.

8 After you take your medicine, you should start to feel much better!

Sometimes a doctor will say you need to go to hospital to see an expert, called a consultant, who will be able to help you even more. They are special experts for different bits of your body.

7 When the doctor has found out what is wrong, you might get a prescription. This is for medicine to help you. Your adult will go to a pharmacy to get your medicine.

When was the last time you had to go to the doctor?

Who took you there?

Did you get any medicine?

How did you feel afterward?

27

Going to the Dentist

We all need to keep our teeth healthy. That's why it's important to go to the dentist. The dentist knows all about teeth. They can check your teeth are healthy, spot problems early, help with crooked teeth, and make sure any teeth problems don't get worse.

Here's what to expect

1 Your adult will make an appointment for you.

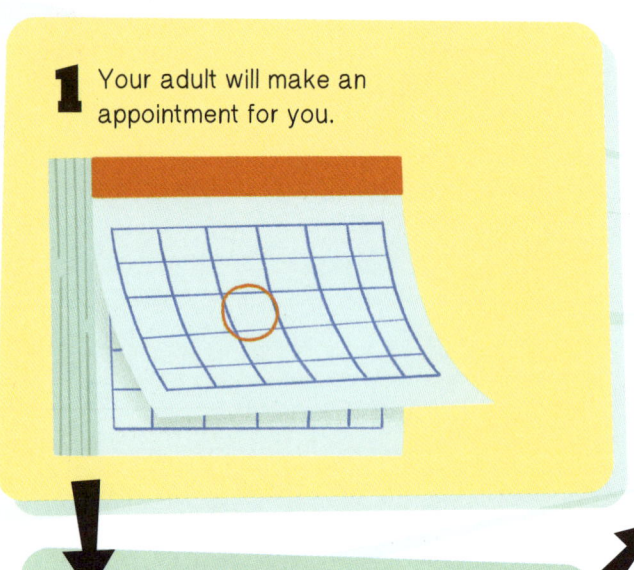

2 You can take music or your phone with you, if it helps you to relax.

3 A receptionist will greet you and check to see if the dentist is ready to see you. You may have to wait in a waiting room.

Keep track of your tooth health for a week. Check the boxes as you go.

MON	TUES
AM: Teeth brushed	AM: Teeth brushed
❌	❌
PM: Teeth brushed	PM: Teeth brushed

4 The dentist will welcome you into their room. There will be bright lights, so the dentist can see clearly into your mouth. You sit on a special chair that the dentist can adjust to get the best view of your teeth. There may be something for you to look at on the ceiling, while the checkup is happening.

5 The dentist uses special tools to check your teeth and gums. They don't hurt.

6 If your teeth are all okay, the dentist will tell you and you may get a sticker.

7 If there are problems with your teeth, the dentist will explain what they are and your adult will make another appointment to come back and get them fixed.

It's really important you brush your teeth and don't eat too many sweets or drink too many fizzy drinks. These can cause problems with your teeth.

WED	THURS	FRI	SAT	SUN
AM: Teeth brushed	AM: Teeth brushed	AM: Teeth brushed	AM: Teeth brushed	AM: Teeth brushed
❌	❌	❌	❌	❌
PM: Teeth brushed	PM: Teeth brushed	PM: Teeth brushed	PM: Teeth brushed	PM: Teeth brushed

Going to the Optometrist

Our eyes are amazing! That's why we need to look after them.

Tell your adult if you:

- ☑ Get lots of headaches
- ☑ Find it hard to read
- ☑ Can't read the board at school
- ☑ Rub your eyes a lot
- ☑ Need to sit near to the TV or computer screen

If you do experience any of these things, you may need to go to an optometrist. Optometrists look after your eyesight. They will check your eyes to make sure they're healthy. They'll also see if you need to wear glasses to help you see.

What to expect at the optometrist

You will sit in a special chair facing a board. The room will be made darker. Your adult can sit next to you. On the board the optometrist may put pictures or letters. These will get smaller in size. They will ask you to tell them what you see.

If they think you need help, they will put special glasses on you. They can put things called "lenses" into the glasses. Sometimes these lenses will make you see clearly and sometimes they will be blurry. Tell the optician what you see.

If the lenses help, your optometrist might suggest you need glasses.

They will let you choose what frames you like for the glasses. And they will measure your face to get an exact fit.

Once the glasses have been specially made for you, the optometrist will tell you so you can pick them up. They might take a few days to be made up.

Look after your glasses using the case your optometrist gives you. Remember to wear them to keep your eyes happy and healthy!

Do you wear glasses?

Draw your ideal set of frames in the box below.

Going to Hospital

Sometimes you are too sick for your doctor to help you. Then you will go to hospital. Your adult may take you, or in an emergency you might go in an ambulance.

There are lots of different departments in a hospital, and experts who look after different bits of your body. If you have an eye problem, you'll see an eye doctor. If you have a skin problem, you'll see a skin doctor. In an emergency, you will go to the ER. ER stands for "Emergency Room."

Sometimes you might have to stay overnight in hospital. It might feel a little scary, but there are lots of people to look after you. There will also be other children there, as well as lots of games to play and TV to watch.

You might get medicine to help you. You may have an operation, too. Soon you will start to feel much better. When you are better, you can go home.

You may have to come back to hospital, but now you know where you're going and who you'll see. And you know it's all to help you feel better.

Remember: you can always talk to a grown-up about anything that's worrying you.

Have you ever had to go to hospital? Write about it below.

Who did you go with?

Did you have anything done, like an injection or an X-ray?

Did you stay overnight? What was it like?

Did you bring any toys or games with you? Did they have any there?

How did you feel?

Did you speak to any doctors or nurses?

Did you take any medicine?

How did you feel when you went home afterward?

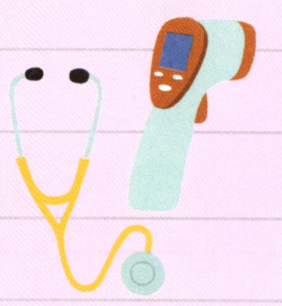

Taking Medicines

Sometimes when you're ill, you need to take medicines. This can be a liquid you swallow, pills you take, ointment or cream you rub on, or medicine you dissolve in water. Often you take medicines for a set time over several days or even longer.

Some people have to take medicine regularly all their life. This could be because they have a problem that can't be cured, but can be managed. Maybe you or your friend have one of these problems, like asthma, diabetes, or eczema?

Can you find the following?

medicine, pill, swallow, inhaler, asthma, diabetes, cream

Wordsearch

I	A	M	A	P	A	L	N	M	O	S	H
N	M	E	D	I	C	I	N	E	A	W	E
H	A	D	A	L	A	R	G	P	C	A	G
A	S	T	H	L	I	A	E	T	A	L	W
L	F	C	A	S	T	H	M	A	P	L	N
E	A	G	A	H	P	O	A	I	M	O	P
R	A	D	I	A	B	E	T	E	S	W	A

34

"I've had eczema since I was a baby. I get it all over my body. It's so itchy. Sometimes I can't help scratching. Mom and I put ointment on my body twice a day. It can take ages and be annoying, but I know it's helping. If it gets really bad, we have to go to the doctor and get medicine. The doctors say I might grow out of it as I get older."

Ben, aged 11, eczema

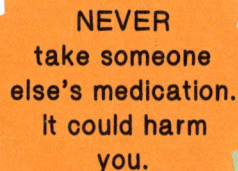

NEVER take someone else's medication. It could harm you.

"When I was about 5, I had problems with going to the toilet. I had to have an operation. Now I have an opening on my body with a pouch attached to it. This is where my poop goes. It has to be emptied several times a day. My school are really understanding and I always have an adult to help me. My friends asked about it a few times, but now they don't really care!"

Noah, aged 12, stoma

"When I was 8, I started to feel tired all the time. I got a lot of headaches and had bruises that I didn't remember getting. Dad took me to the doctors and I had to go to hospital for them to do some tests. They said it was diabetes. My body can't control how much sugar goes into my blood very well. I had to learn what I could and couldn't eat. I also learned to test myself. If I need to, I can inject myself with the medicine I need. I'm proud of what I have achieved. Nothing is going to stop me. I know I am brave."

Emily, aged 10, diabetes

35

Help! 911!
IN AN EMERGENCY, CALL 911

CALLING 911

In an emergency like a fire, a dangerous crime, or when someone is seriously hurt, you can call 911.

Most importantly, make sure you are somewhere safe **FIRST**. A person on the line will ask you if you want the fire department, police, or an ambulance. Ask for the one you need.

Speak as clearly and as calmly as you can, but don't worry if you're upset. You will be asked what happened. You might be asked if someone is conscious, which means awake. You might also be asked if they're breathing. You can see this from their chest moving up and down, or you can put your hand on their chest to check.

If you're at home, give the emergency service your home address, including the zipcode. Make sure you know it. If you're out, look around at street names and shops, so you can describe where you are near.

DON'T hang up until the emergency service arrives. Be prepared to let them in if you're at home.

DON'T call 911 as a joke. You may stop people from getting the help they need. It is also against the law.

DON'T be scared about calling. 911 is used to taking calls from children and will help you.

TEST YOURSELF

1. What number do you call in an emergency?
  a. 123
  b. 911
  c. Your home number

2. When you call 911, the first question will be?
  a. Your name
  b. Your age
  c. Fire, police, or ambulance

3. You may be asked, "is the person conscious?" If someone is conscious, they are:
  a. Hurt
  b. Breathing
  c. Awake

4. How can you tell if someone is breathing?
  a. Move them
  b. See if their chest is moving up and down
  c. See if their eyes are open

5. After you call an ambulance, you should:
  a. Stay on the line until they arrive
  b. Hang up immediately
  c. It doesn't matter when you put the phone down

6. Should you call the ambulance if you want a ride home?
  a. No
  b. Yes
  c. Not sure

(Answers: 1b, 2c, 3c, 4b, 5a, 6a)

Basic First Aid

Sometimes you might hurt yourself, but it might not be serious. Here's how to treat common problems. Always ask an adult to help.

CUT If you've cut yourself, perhaps on paper or with some scissors, carefully clean the wound with water. Pat it dry. Put a bandage over the cut.

GRAZE If you graze yourself, it's important to make sure that your cut is free of grit or dirt. Run it under water until it's completely clean. You may like to add antiseptic cream. If you're not using a bandage, you could use some gauze and medical tape. A first aid kit has these in it.

STING If a bee or wasp stings you, it can really hurt. When bees sting, they can leave a part of their sting behind. Scrape it out with something flat. Don't pinch or pull, as you might pump more venom into yourself. Use some insect-bite cream.

Some people are allergic to insect stings and need special treatment. If someone you know has trouble breathing after being stung, get an adult to help immediately.

BURN For minor burns, run cool water over the affected area until it stops stinging. Ask your adult for pain relief.

BRUISE Gently apply an ice pack. Your adult could also gently apply lotion to the bruise.

BLISTER Blisters happen where something rubs against your skin. Don't pop blisters, because they are like a cushion, protecting your skin. Blisters will gradually go down, as long as they're left alone.

STAY FRESH!

Keeping ourselves clean is an important part of staying healthy. How fresh are you? Take the quiz to find out!

1. What should you do if you have a runny nose?

　a. Tell everyone.

　b. Wipe it on your sleeve.

　c. Wipe your nose on a tissue and throw it in the trash.

2. What should you do when you cough?

　a. Spread it around.

　b. Do it loudly.

　c. Cover your mouth.

3. How often should you brush your teeth?

　a. When you feel like it.

　b. After every meal.

　c. At least twice per day, in the morning and at night.

4. When should you wash your hands?

　a. Once a week.

　b. When you're told to.

　c. As often as necessary.

5. Why should you trim your nails?

　a. To make them look nice.

　b. To make texting easier.

　c. Dirt under nails can make you ill.

MOSTLY A: You are fond of your germs and like sharing them around! Try to be a bit more fresh!

MOSTLY B: You try to be clean sometimes, but there's room for improvement.

MOSTLY C: Well done! You know that staying fresh keeps you and those around you healthy!

WHAT SHOULD YOU DO AT BEDTIME?
Check the ones you agree with:

☐ Put on pajamas
☐ Go to the bathroom
☐ Wash hands
☐ Get dry
☐ Wash your face or have a bath or shower
☐ Brush teeth

If you checked ALL of them, you're right!

Bad for Bodies: Cigarettes

Smoking cigarettes causes serious damage to your body. Cigarettes are made of crushed, dry tobacco leaves. They contain an addictive chemical called nicotine. Once your body starts taking in nicotine, it keeps wanting more. This means that it's very hard to stop smoking, even though it can kill you. That's why it's best to never even start!

As well as nicotine, tobacco smoke has over 5,000 chemicals in it. Lots of them are poisonous and nearly 100 cause cancer. They include tar (sticky goo that gets in your lungs), arsenic (used in rat poison), benzene (made from crude oil), ethanol (used in anti-freeze), carbon monoxide (found in car exhaust fumes) and ammonia (used for explosives). Cigarettes are also really expensive!

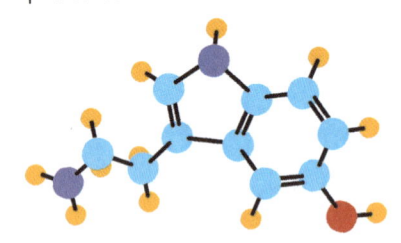

Nicotine molecule

Tobacco plant

Vaping is a way of getting nicotine without smoking cigarettes. It avoids some of the dangerous chemicals from smoking, but it is still bad for you, and extremely addictive.

Smoking can damage a healthy body. On the outside, it may make a person look more wrinkled with yellow fingers and teeth, as well as having bad breath and decaying teeth. On the inside, it can lead to lung disease, eye problems, heart attacks, strokes, and lots of different types of cancer.

Cigarettes have lots of names. You might have heard of ciggies, roll-ups, baccy, cigars, or smokes. Lots of people start smoking to relax, but the opposite is true! Smoking can make you feel more anxious and makes your heart work harder.

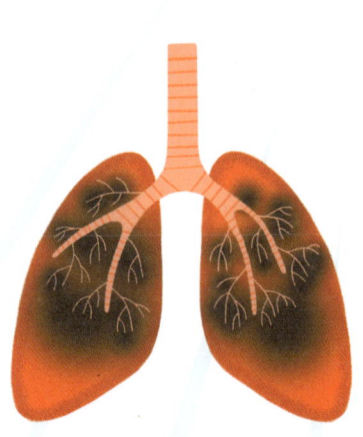

Smoking damages your heart and lungs

Test your knowledge of cigarettes!

1. Which of these is used in antifreeze?

   a. nicotine

   b. carbon monoxide

   c. ethanol

2. What's another word for "makes you crave it"?

   a. addictive

   b. expensive

   c. relative

3. Which of these diseases can you NOT get from smoking?

   a. lung disease

   b. cancer

   c. tennis elbow

4. What's the name of the sticky goo in cigarettes that gets into your lungs?

   a. tar

   b. asphalt

   c. oil

5. How many chemicals are there in tobacco smoke?

   a. 50

   b. 500

   c. 5,000

6. What color does cigarette smoke turn smokers' teeth and nails?

   a. green

   b. yellow

   c. pink

> If you are feeling pressured to try smoking, talk to someone you trust. If someone is pressuring you to do things that are harmful to your health, they are not being a real friend.

Answers: 1. c; 2. a; 3. c; 4. a; 5. c; 6. b

Bad for Bodies: Alcohol

You've probably seen people around you drinking alcohol, maybe at a celebration, like Christmas or someone's birthday. Or perhaps people in your family drink at the end of the day or week.

Alcohol can be split into different types, such as beer, wine, and spirits. Each has different colors, tastes, and strengths.

All alcohol has a BIG effect on your body. Some types of alcohol can be stronger than others. The strength of alcohol is measured by "proof", a number as a percentage you can find on a bottle of alcohol. It's also measured in "units." The higher the number, the stronger it is. A glass of whisky or rum is much stronger than the same sized glass of beer. That means it'll affect your body much more quickly and more obviously.

In It's illegal for under-21s to buy alcohol. That's because your body is still growing and developing. For adults, doctors recommend people stick within a certain limit. That's because alcohol can damage your health in lots of different ways.

Remember: you can always talk to a grown-up about anything you're worried about.

Other drugs exist, which are illegal and can really hurt you. Don't touch them, and tell a grown-up if someone tries to get you or your friends to take them.

42

Can you match up the following labels with the body? They're all effects of too much alcohol. Each label can be used more than once.

A. Brain
B. Mouth and throat
C. Heart
D. Stomach
E. Liver
F. Intestines
G. Armpits
H. Knees

1. Causes bleeding and ulcers (sores)
2. Diarrhea
3. Loss of appetite
4. Vomiting
5. Hard to concentrate
6. Makes joints ache
7. Liver stops working
8. Sweating
9. Causes cancer
10. Irritates stomach
11. Makes heart work harder
12. Risky decisions

Answers: A5 & 12; B 1 & 9; C11; D3, 4 & 10; E7 & 9; F2 & 9; G8; H6

Disability

There are many kinds of disability. A person has a disability when they can't do something the same way an able-bodied person can. Some disabilities are easy to see, like when someone can't walk or uses a wheelchair. And some are hidden or much harder to see, like when someone finds it hard to think clearly.

Some people have disabilities from the day they're born. Other people may have them because of a disease or accident later in life. There are lots of different types of disability, and people manage them in lots of different ways.

Jodie had a disease that damaged her ears about a year ago. She used to be able to hear fine, but now she has special hearing aids. She's learning sign language, and so are her friends.

Billy's in a wheelchair. He finds it hard to control his body. His body jerks, even when he doesn't want it to. He has an amazing sense of humor and loves to tell jokes.

Ava was in an accident when she was a baby. She lost her leg. Now she has a prosthetic limb where her leg used to be. She loves going to gymnastics, but can be a bit shy in new places.

"LIKE STARS IN THE SKY, WE WERE BORN TO SHINE"
Andrea Bocelli

Think about what you do during the day at school. Now imagine Billy, Jodie, and Ava are joining your school. What might they find easy? What might they find hard? How could you help make things easier?

	What they might find easy	What they might find hard	How I could help
Billy			
Ava			
Jodie			

Disabled, but able!

Just because someone has a disability doesn't mean they can't dream big! Here are some famous people, who didn't let their disability stand in their way.

Frida Kahlo became a world-famous artist. She suffered from polio in her childhood and had lifelong health problems.

John Forbes Nash Jr. was a world-famous mathematician, who won a Nobel Prize. He suffered from a severe mental illness.

Professor Stephen Hawking was a legendary scientist. He had a disease that caused paralysis and used a machine to write and speak.

Andrea Bocelli is a famous musician. He became completely blind after a football accident aged 12.

Aaron Fotheringham is a famous skater. He was the first person to do a complete somersault off a ramp in his wheelchair.

Billie Eilish is a famous pop star. She has Tourette syndrome, a condition that makes her face twitch.

Ryan Gosling is a Hollywood actor. He has ADHD (Attention deficit hyperactivity disorder).

Muhammed Ali was a legendary boxer. He had dyslexia.

Bethany Hamilton is a world-famous surfer. When she was 13, a shark bit off her arm. It didn't stop her becoming a professional athlete.

WONDERFUL ME

Draw a picture of yourself in the box below.

Now list five things you like about your body. It could be something about your appearance, like the color of your eyes. Or it could be something your body is really good at, like doing gymnastics.

1

2

3

4

5

Hopefully by now you will realize:

☑ How amazing your body is

☑ How to keep it amazing

Now it's time to commit to healthy, happy you.

Choose THREE things that can help you to stay healthy. For example: playing football after school, eating healthy, drinking more water, or getting enough sleep.

1. I will_____
_____

2. I will_____
_____

3. I will_____
_____
_____

I CAN DO THIS!

HELP!

If you ever need help with something, and you don't have a grown-up you can talk to, there are lots of places you can go for help. Don't ever feel bad or guilty for asking for more information or support. These resources are there to help you.

Online resources

www.nutrition.gov/topics/nutrition-age/children
Activities, recipes, and advice about healthy eating and physical activity

www.cdc.gov/ncbddd/kids
Lots of information about different types of disability, as well as quizzes and activities. They also have lists of books and movies about people who live with different kinds of disability

www.cdc.gov/bam
Learn about health and fitness, including information about diseases, healthy eating, and keeping active.

Trusted adults

If you'd rather not talk to your parents about something, you may want to speak to other trusted adults in your life. This might be:

- an older relative,
- a teacher,
- a school counselor,
- your school nurse,
- your doctor or nurse,
- a sexual health clinician,
- your therapist,
- a youth worker or social worker.

You know best who you feel comfortable talking to.

In an emergency or life-threatening situation,

call 911.

If there is a grown-up around who you trust, ask them to make the call.

ONLY STRONG PEOPLE ASK FOR HELP